MW00535331

SHEPHERDS IN
THE FIELDS

SHEPHERDS IN THE FIELDS

Susan B. Wells

What Others Are Saying about
Shepherds in the Fields

For too long Christians have promoted the unbiblical idea that "ministers" are only those who stand behind a pulpit on Sunday mornings. This limited concept has crippled us. Sadly, many believers forget that the Bible says we're all "ministers of reconciliation" (2 Corinthians 5:18). Whether we're elementary school teachers, mechanics, students, waitresses, executives, flight attendants, accountants, or full-time preachers, every Christian has a sphere of influence. It's our job as witnesses of Christ to shine His light in the marketplace.

Susan Wells knows this because she has served as both a pastor and a health care provider. She knows God has given her a "field" to care for, and that every believer has a similar stewardship. I'm so glad she's sharing this vital message with a larger audience. I pray that as you study the concepts in this book and answer the questions at the end of each chapter, God will remind you, that you, too, have a holy calling, no matter what your job is. Your vocation is from God, and it comes with great responsibility. I pray the Lord will open your eyes to see how He has uniquely equipped you to be a witness for Him in your workplace.

J. Lee Grady
Author, *Set My Heart on Fire* and *10 Lies the Church Tells Women*
Director, The Mordecai Project

I wondered what more I could learn about the familiar Christmas story. Susan Wells pleasantly surprised me. She looked at a very familiar phrase from a different angle, then took me on a wonderful journey to reevaluate my life and priorities. This book is a refreshing and much needed spiritual checkup. I suspect it will be good for you, too.

Eddie Smith, Worldwide Publishing Group

Shepherds in the Fields
©2021 by Susan B. Wells

All rights reserved.

Scripture quotations, unless otherwise noted, are taken from the New American Standard Bible® (NASB), Copyright © 1960, 1962, 1963, 1968, 1971, 1972, 1973, 1975, 1977, 1995, 2020 by The Lockman Foundation. Used by permission (www.Lockman.org).

Scripture quotations marked KJV are taken from the King James Bible, Public Domain.

Scripture quotations marked NKJV are taken from the New King James Version®. Copyright © 1982 by Thomas Nelson, Inc. Used by permission. All rights reserved.

Scripture quotations marked NIV are taken from THE HOLY BIBLE, NEW INTERNATIONAL VERSION®, NIV® Copyright © 1973, 1978, 1984, 2011 by Biblica, Inc.™ Used by permission. All rights reserved worldwide.

Scripture quotations marked NLT are taken from the Holy Bible, New Living Translation copyright © 1996, 2004, 2007 by Tyndale House Foundation. Used by permission of Tyndale House Publishers Inc., Carol Stream, IL 60188. All rights reserved. New Living, NLT, and the New Living Translation logo are registered trademarks of Tyndale House Publishers.

Cover design by Wise Designs

ISBN: 978-0-9910310-2-3 (paperback)
ISBN: 978-0-9910310-3-0 (ebook)
Author's photograph by Falero Studios

To my sweet Dennis, the one who tells me,
"I believe you can do anything."
I'll love you forever.

Acknowledgments

First, I want to thank the Lord for patiently prodding me to write this book. I began working on it several years ago, but laid it down, thinking the task was too great. I figured, *surely somebody else will write it!* When I was furloughed for four months during the pandemic of 2020, the Lord spoke to me, "Remember how you said you don't have time to write the book? Well *now* you do."

I'm also truly thankful for my family's understanding when I had to devote so much time to writing. Dennis, your continued support, prayer coverage, and belief in me are blessings I treasure. I look forward to wonderful, distraction-free time with you all . . . especially my grands!

My heart overflows with gratitude for the wonderful gift of friends. They've been a real source of encouragement, challenging me to put on paper the message I've "preached" to them. Among this group is my precious editor, Lori Hatcher, who has patiently and lovingly held my hand and guided me through the process of writing.

I am abundantly blessed with opportunities to "shepherd" my patients and those with whom I'm honored to serve. Partnering with the Good Shepherd in the field of medicine brings me incredible joy.

Finally, I'm thankful for the gift of my parents, Ted and Anne Bailey. Never underestimate the eternal investment you've made in my life. The older I get, the more I cherish you.

~Susan Wells

Contents

Foreword

SUSAN WELLS DOESN'T JUST WRITE about how to be a shepherd in the field, she lives it. Almost a decade ago I sat in her office for my annual checkup. I assumed we were done when she finished the lab tests and exam, but then she asked two questions.

"How are you doing?" and "Is there anything else you'd like to talk about?"

Her genuine concern unlocked the flood of tears I'd been hiding behind my brave face.

She listened patiently as I described my heartbreak, then shared a page from her family's story. Coming alongside me in my grief, she spoke truth—just one verse from God's Word—that turned my upside-down world right side up again.

Susan demonstrated how we can reach out to the people God has placed in our "fields" and speak words of life and hope. We can inspire and encourage them through our life experiences, our faith journey, and our knowledge of God's Word.

She could have provided the medical care I needed and sent me on my way, but she went one step further. She looked past my physical body and touched my soul. She entered into my storm and tossed me a life preserver—one I clung to all the way through my trial until the sun shone again.

Susan didn't ask me to endorse her book. I asked her. I believe in her message because I've experienced what happens when Christians shepherd the fields where God has placed them. I can only imagine what God could do with an army of shepherds just like her.

~Lori Hatcher
Author of *Refresh Your Faith, Uncommon Devotions from Every Book of the Bible*

Introduction

As I FINISHED MY LAST clinical rotations in Physician Assistant (PA) school, I eagerly anticipated graduating in the summer of 2008. I couldn't wait to begin my new career. Reading through the New Testament for the umpteenth time, my Scripture passage for the day included Luke 2:1-20 (NKJV). We know this passage as "The Christmas Story."

As I read the familiar passage (and thought of Christmas six months away), I felt as though the Lord highlighted the words ". . . Now there were in the same country *shepherds living out in the fields keeping watch over their flock by night.*" The familiar scene painted itself in my mind: shepherds, sheep, sleeping under the stars, fighting off the predators stalking their prey in the darkness. Oftentimes when I read the Bible, I see it like a movie. I feel as though I'm there, watching the stories unfold. On this occasion, however, I saw this scene from a different perspective.

Merriam-Webster Online Dictionary offers several definitions for the word *field*. Here are a few: 1. an area of cleared enclosed land used for cultivation or pasture (this one usually comes to mind when we read the passage in Luke 2:8), 2. the place where a battle is fought, or 3. an area or division of an activity, subject, or profession.[1] For the purpose of this introduction, and to encourage us in our workplace ministry,

I'd like to focus on the last definition – "an area or division of an activity, subject, or profession."[2]

Picture the shepherds in their fields keeping watch over their flocks. Imagine what would happen if every Christ-follower viewed their place of employment, home, and community as their field. What if they saw everyone they encountered as part of the flock they were to shepherd?

It's a radical thought but think how quickly a mindset like this would enable us to evangelize the world! Not only that, but good tidings would be preached to the poor, broken hearts would be healed, liberty would be proclaimed to the captives, the prison doors of those who are bound would be opened, and the acceptable year of the Lord (His favor) would be proclaimed (Isaiah 61:1-2 NKJV).

This is the picture I saw in my mind's eye that hot June day in 2008—the concept of believers living as "shepherds living in the fields" to minister to and evangelize our world. The notion of "marketplace ministry" made us aware of the mission field the workplace provides, but it doesn't go far enough. We need to embrace more fully the mandates in Mark 16:15 (KJV) to "go ye into *all* the world," (including the marketplace and everywhere else we frequent) and "make disciples" (Matthew 28:19).

The time has come when the Lord is calling all His people to view whatever "area or division of an activity, subject, or profession"[3] as their *field* and themselves as *shepherds* in those fields. This next level defines that ministry as more of a "shepherding" approach in the workplace, thereby allowing us to reach others for Christ and minister to the Body of Christ that we come in contact with in our "fields."

I've lived out this vision in my professional life as a Physician Assistant and in my personal life as a wife, mother, church member, neighbor, and citizen. I invite you to explore how walking as a shepherd in our field should be not only what we do, but who we are. Functioning this way should be a natural outflow of the Life of God that lives in us because of our ongoing relationship with Jesus Christ. It's an exciting way to live!

If you're a Christ-follower who wants to impact this broken world with the love of God and the eternal life He offers, I invite you to journey with me.

CHAPTER 1
The Shepherding Approach

THE CONCEPT OF MINISTRY in the marketplace isn't a new one. Over the last 30+ years, Christians have become increasingly aware of the reality and validity of this rich mission field. Ministries have arisen to enlighten and equip believers to "Go ye therefore into all the world" (Mark 16:15 KJV), especially the work world.

Workplace ministry has become a common theme of best-selling books and a major topic of discussion at Christian conferences. At the 2004 Lausanne Committee for World Evangelization meeting, an impressive document was published addressing the various ways and means to facilitate this. Speakers encouraged the Body of Christ to embrace workplace ministry as a tool to evangelize the world.

While I fully embrace the concept of workplace ministry, I believe the Great Commission is much broader than what happens between the hours of 9-5. It embraces every aspect of our life. Wherever we find ourselves—home, work, church, social settings, even the grocery store—can be the setting for kingdom work.

If we want to impact people for God's kingdom, we must see them as God sees them—as sheep. And we must see our lives as "fields" where the sheep live.

God describes people as sheep in Isaiah 53:6: "All of us like sheep have gone astray."

Because God created people with many of the characteristics of sheep, if we want to reach sheep, we must meet their needs. What are these needs? The basics are obvious: air, water, food, shelter, and companionship. To gain these necessities, sheep need someone to oversee their care. Because they're helpless and unable to provide for and defend themselves, they need a shepherd. Without one, they will die.

The Duties of a Shepherd

What does a shepherd do? He watches over the sheep and lives among them to identify with them and gain their trust. Because he knows them intimately, he can lead them to green pastures, defend them from would-be predators, provide healing for the wounded and sick, and seek and pursue those that are lost. This sounds similar to what the Father modeled for us through His Son Jesus, doesn't it?

Luke 2:8 (NKJV) provides the genesis of this shepherding approach to ministry in the workplace: "Now there were in the same country shepherds living out (abiding) in the fields, keeping watch over their flock by night." As we look at the language of this passage and the definitions in the Greek language in which it was written, we can more clearly appreciate this concept.

The word "shepherd" is the word, *poimen*.[1] It speaks of "he to whose care and control others have committed themselves, and whose precepts they follow."[2] God calls Christians to function as "shepherds" in whatever "field" He has placed us.

We don't have to have an official title to operate as a shepherd. Remember, *shepherd* is both a noun *and* a verb. If you are "shepherding," then you *are* a shepherd! Like with all ministry gifts, specifically the five-fold ones that include apostles, prophets, evangelists, pastors (sometimes referred to as "shepherds"), and teachers seen in Ephesians 4:11, a person will function as at least one of these in their actions (verb), before they are labeled as one (noun).

For example, a person shouldn't call themself an evangelist if he hasn't been "evangelizing" (doing the work that an evangelist does naturally, flowing out of the way they're gifted and wired by the Creator). I knew a young minister who believed he was called to be an evangelist, but during all the years I'd observed his ministry, he'd never personally led anyone to the Lord. He hadn't witnessed to anyone, nor had he been involved in an evangelistic outreach.

There's no greater joy than being who God created you to be. Conversely, there's no greater frustration than trying to be something you're not.

The shepherds in this passage were "keeping watch." The word "keeping" is the Greek word, *phylasso*.[3] Its definition contains the idea of "guarding, protection, observance, and caring for."[4] The word "watch" is the word *phylake*.[5] It's derived from the previously mentioned word for "keeping." In English, we'd translate this phrase, *keep keeping*. It conveys the image of "a guard or sentinel," and it speaks "of the time (of night) during which guard was kept; a period of time during which a guard was on duty."[6] This framework underscores the fact that sheep are vulnerable creatures and need someone to guard and protect them.

Where Is My Field?

As a Physician Assistant, when I view my place of employment through the lens of shepherding, I can clearly see God has given me the responsibility of guarding what has been entrusted to my care. I accomplish this by observing those with whom I come in daily contact and for whom I provide care.

My patients come to me with a physical or emotional need. I listen to them and determine the best course of action to promote their wellbeing. I may suggest lab work, studies, tests, medication, or surgical management. Sometimes I provide much-needed reassurance.

But what if you don't oversee direct patient care or work in such an obvious care-giving role? You may say, "I'm not a PA. I'm a teacher, or I'm a cashier at a grocery store, or I ride on a sanitation truck and collect garbage. How am I supposed to function as a shepherd in my field?"

Excellent question! Everyone, unless you live alone in a hut on top of a mountain, crosses paths with other people, *sheep* if you will, on a regular basis.

Suppose you're a fifth-grade teacher. You oversee a classroom filled with "lambs." You have the privilege of watching over them for several hours a day, Monday through Friday throughout the school year. You arrive in the classroom before they do, right? Why not take a few moments before they arrive to walk by each desk, pray for, and declare a blessing over each student represented? When they come to your desk for help or to ask a question, show the love of the Father in the way you respond to them. Demonstrate that you care.

If you're a cashier at a local grocery store, you have insight into the needs of your customer's lives. If they buy cold medicine, someone in their household is probably sick and could use prayer for healing. If you see them buying diapers or formula, there's probably a baby in the house. Pray for the Lord to bless their children and meet every need they have.

I don't suggest you interact in an in an overly familiar or inappropriate manner with customers. In most cases, your prayers should be quick, to the point, and silent—a conversation between you and God. With rare exceptions, it's not the time or place for you to initiate a prayer meeting. Remember, you have a responsibility to your employer be a loyal, hardworking employee. (More on this in an upcoming chapter.)

If you work for the sanitation department, you have the privilege of passing by homes and businesses every day. Why not offer up prayer for the people living and working in these buildings? Ask the Lord to bless them and meet their needs. Your prayers don't have to be long or lengthy to be effective. God hears the prayers of those who will "stand in the gap" for others and intercede.

Years ago, when my husband and I pastored a local church, I led the ministry of intercession. I'd often take some of our intercessors into the neighborhood that surrounded our church. We'd pile into my van and drive around praying for each of the homes and the people who lived in them. I called those opportunities, "drive-by prayings."

This perspective of shepherding in the fields where God has placed us can change the way we see our position in our workplace. When we look through shepherds' eyes, we realize the time we spend working is not just about punching a timecard, working our shift, and leaving. It's about guarding the "sheep" in our spheres of influence and responsibility each day. Wow! Every minute of our life is about the sheep God has placed in our field.

Timing Is Everything

Keep in mind that the timing of our ministry is vital. Note when the shepherds were watching their sheep. Luke 2:8 says they were, "keeping watch over their flock by *night.*" The Greek word *nyx*[7] describes the time when sheep most need a shepherd's eye. The word contains in its definition a "metaphor for the time when work ceases; time for deeds of sin and shame; time of moral stupidity and darkness; time when the weary and also the drunken give themselves up to slumber."[8]

Shepherds watch their flock most carefully during times of vulnerability. Human sheep also need special care during times of weakness. The people around you might need you to watch over them with extra vigilance: when they've completed a project that's consumed a large quantity of time, attention, and energy; when they're presented with a temptation to sin (sins of opportunity); when they're physically weary; when they're under the influence of something that affects their ability to think clearly (a substance, a something, or a someone); when they're in the dark because of their or someone else's choices; or during a time when they're just being plain *stupid.*

Our Field Goes Beyond Our Workplace

As we discussed earlier, the word "fields" can include "an area or division of an activity, subject, or profession."[9] Our "fields" of influence or ministry aren't limited to workplace opportunities, nor are they limited to our eight-hour workday. They also include "an area or division of an activity"[10] we frequent.

For example, I shop at Wal Mart at least once a week. Wal Mart is one of my fields. I encounter needy sheep there all the time. I'm not advocating that you stalk people to minister to them. Quite the contrary.

While I shop, my attention may be drawn to a particular person or circumstance. I might see a stressed-out mother shopping with her children in tow (this brings back memories for me of that season in my life). I can pray for her to have grace in this precious, and, I might add *brief,* season. That she may view being a mother as a noble position of honor, and see the children she's been given as precious gifts from God. I'd pray she'd have the grace to perceive and accomplish her vital calling to "train them up in the way they should go" (Proverbs 22:6).

When we realize we're God's ambassador and, consequently, His shepherd in the fields, wherever we go, we'll find sheep who desperately need to be "touched" by the Great Shepherd through us. Imagine how quickly we could reach the world for Christ and how His Kingdom could be manifest in the earth if we approached all of life and the world in which we live with this vision!

Points to Ponder:
1. Can you identify your field? Where is it?
2. Who or what does the Lord want you to "keep watch over" in your field?
3. What are some practical ways you can incorporate a shepherding approach in your field?

CHAPTER 2

The Garden Assignment

NOW THAT WE UNDERSTAND the New Testament application of shepherding, let's turn to the Old Testament for another look at this concept. In Genesis 2:15, we see the shepherding approach illustrated with Adam in the Garden of Eden. "Then the Lord God took the man and put him in the garden (field) of Eden to cultivate and keep it." By studying the Hebrew definitions of a few key words, we can extract and understand God's original intent.

The word "took" comes from the Hebrew word, *laqach*, which conveys the picture of acquiring, marrying, or taking a wife.[1] It reveals God's commitment to Adam before Adam knew or had committed himself to God. In these words, we see glimmers of a truth that's woven through the Bible: God is *always* the initiator of commitment.

Paul references this in Romans 5:8, "But God demonstrates His own love toward us, in that while we were yet sinners, Christ died for us." Jesus, the lover of our soul, paid the ultimate price for us, so He could *acquire* us before we ever knew Him or knew we needed Him. God's commitment to us serves as an example of how we should commit ourselves to the field we shepherd.

After God "took" Adam, He then "put" (*nuwach*), which means "to rest, settle down and remain in the garden."[2] "Garden" (*gan*) depicts an "enclosure, enclosed garden, which is figurative of a bride."[3] Isn't it interesting that after God committed to Adam, He then required Adam to be committed to and remain and rest where He placed him, much like a husband is committed to his bride. (Spoiler Alert: No bride wants to be married to a *restless* and *uncommitted* man!)

It's also interesting to note that the word "garden," pictured as an *enclosed* area implies that it has defined and established boundaries, with *finite*, not infinite, responsibilities. When the Lord commissions us to an area or region, He *always* defines the borders.

We see this over and over again in Old Testament passages about the assigned sections of the Promised Land God gave to each tribe of Israel. He delineated the borders of their individual territories. As shepherds in our fields, God desires us to operate the same way.

How Boundaries Help Us

As a Physician Assistant, I'm responsible for shepherding in my office and with my patients. I don't have the responsibility or designated authority to walk into the hospital that employs me and exercise authority over another healthcare provider's patients. I know my limits, and I believe they've been established by the Lord. If at some time He chooses to enlarge my borders, He can do that in a way that others will recognize as valid.

Having defined boundaries over our responsibilities protects us from burn out. Acting within my designated authority by only assuming responsibility within my assignment and not trying to be or do something I'm not called or equipped for enables me to walk in freedom. I won't struggle under a false or improper sense of responsibility.

God's boundaries also provide protection against Satan, the enemy of our soul. Oftentimes, if he can't stop us from doing God's will for our life, he'll try to destroy us in the midst of doing it. If you're an intercessor, for example, he'll try to overwhelm you with prayer burdens. He'll flood your mind with so many issues you won't feel there are enough hours in the day to pray about them. You'll either burn out, give up, quit, or become deceived and experience a moral failure. If we allow the Lord to define our responsibilities and stay in our "garden," however, we can avoid both. Repeat the phrase, "Boundaries are good," whenever you're tempted to take on more than God requires of you.

Another interesting nugget about the word *gan* is that it's derived from the Hebrew root word *ganan*, which includes the concept of "to hedge about; defending, covering, and surrounding."[4] As believers, God's people have a mandate to protect the place, people, and resources of our assigned region. Ezekiel 22:30 (KJV) clearly illustrates God's position about who's responsible for protecting "the land" when He says, "And I sought for a man among them, that should *make up the hedge*, and stand in the gap before me for the land, that I should not destroy it: but I found none."

This is one of the saddest verses in the Bible. Here the Lord looks for someone to whom He can entrust the assignment of making up a hedge to protect and cover "the land." He doesn't just speak of the earth, but also includes the people who inhabit it. This sounds very much like a shepherding role, doesn't it? Sadly, God found no one to intercede for the nation. May the Lord never make this indictment about the region in which He's placed us.

How Should We Approach Our Assignments?

We also see this shepherding approach to our assignments in the wording used in Genesis 2:15 to describe Adam's responsibilities in the garden. It says God "put him into the garden of Eden to cultivate it and keep it." Let's dig into the original Hebrew words to better understand God's design for the way we should approach our assignments.

Some translations substitute the word "tend" for "cultivate." The original Hebrew word used is *abad*. It means "to work, serve another by labour; to serve God (with Levitical service)."[5] This word can also be translated "worship," as in Exodus 4:23 (NIV), "and I told you, 'Let my son go, so he may *worship (abad)* me.'" Wow! Have you ever realized God equates work with worship? He wants us to live our lives and perform our work as an act of worship to Him.

Paul underscores this mindset in Colossians 3:23, "Whatever you do, do your work heartily, as for the Lord rather than for men." How would you approach your job if you believed your real employer was the Lord?

The word "keep" is the word *shamar*. Its definition includes the image of "hedging about with thorns; to keep guard, watch, protect, save life, preserve."[6] Hedging something with thorns to protect it seems rather extreme, but it implies that what is being protected is precious.

This definition also conveys the understanding that our work is synonymous with our service to God and illustrates the responsibilities given to the Levitical priests regarding the tabernacle of Moses in Numbers 3. Not only were they responsible for representing God to man and man to God, but they served as guardians and protectors over what had been placed under their care.

As Christians, we're called to carry out priestly and guardian responsibilities every day, wherever we go. We've been entrusted by the Lord with precious treasures to "shamar." Oh, that we would see what we do where we work, where we live, and where we frequent as "service to God" with a holy calling upon it!

Pleasure in Service

Lastly, the word *Eden* contains the idea of pleasure in its definition.[7] It comes from the primitive root word, *adan*, which means, "to luxuriate, delight oneself."[8] God, Who is always good, has only the best plans for us. In His infinite love and mercy, He has sovereignly placed each of us in a designated region according to "the counsel of His will" (Ephesians 1:11). He's not a prison warden watching over us while we "do our time" of suffering during our sentence here on earth. On the contrary, Jeremiah 29:11(NLT) reveals He has "plans for good (peace or shalom) and not for disaster, to give you a future and a hope."

His desire is that wherever He places us, we would find delight and pleasure. Notice I said, "find." To find, one must be looking, so we must approach our assignment with the mindset of looking for the delight and pleasure in it.

Proverbs 11:27 (NLT) contains the promise, "If you search for good, you will find favor; but if you search for evil, it will find you!" The gist of this verse is, "whatever you look for in your situation and circumstance, you *will* find." It also underscores the power of our perspectives and our choices upon our life. If your garden is less than the Eden God desires it to be, who's responsible for that?

If you're still not convinced that God holds us responsible for the condition of our regions, here are several more verses that reflect His perspective:

- Second Chronicles 7:14 (NKJV, italics mine) – "If *My people* who are *called by My name* will humble themselves, and pray and seek My face, and turn from their wicked ways, then I will hear from heaven, and will forgive their sin and heal their land."
- Proverbs 11:11 (italics mine) – "By the blessing of *the upright* the city is exalted."
- Romans 8:19, 21 (NKJV, italics mine) – "For the earnest expectation of the creation eagerly waits for the revealing of *the sons of God* . . . For we know that the whole creation groans and labors with birth pangs together until now."

God's Command and Our Responsibility

As we review our key passage in Genesis 2:15, "The Lord God took the man and put him in the garden (field) of Eden to tend (cultivate) and keep it," we're reminded of God's commandment to us and our responsibility concerning our assigned places. It's important to note God gave this commandment *before* the fall, before Adam and Eve sinned, and has *never* rescinded it. It was and still is part of His purpose for mankind.

Remembering that our "gardens" refer to any assigned location, vocation, region, or position where God has placed us, we can extract the following truths:

- We are to be "taken" by the Lord and married to Him first and foremost before we commit to anyone or anything else.
- We are to settle, remain, and have rest in the garden where He's put us.
- We are to defend the garden like a man defends, surrounds, and covers his bride.
- We are to find delight in the garden.
- We are to work/serve the Lord and others in our assigned garden as an act of worship to Him.

Points to Ponder:

1. Who's *really* responsible for the condition of your "garden?"
2. Have you struggled to settle, remain, have rest in, and find delight in your garden?
3. Who or what has been entrusted to you to serve and protect as the Lord Himself would?
4. Have you been working in your garden as unto the Lord and as an act of worship to Him?

CHAPTER 3
The Garden of Redemption

IN THE PREVIOUS CHAPTER we saw a viable example of the shepherding approach in the Old Testament Garden. Now we'll return to the New Testament for an example of how Jesus demonstrated this shepherding method in another Garden.

In Matthew 26:36-45, Jesus restored our place, responsibility, and authority in the garden by what He modeled in the Garden of Gethsemane. We know the first Adam, along with Eve, relinquished their God-given responsibilities to "tend and keep" the Garden of Eden. The second Adam, Jesus Christ, the Son of God, restored us to our rightful place as shepherds by watching over, protecting, defending, and releasing salvation to mankind through His labored intercession in the Garden of Gethsemane.

When We Want to Quit

In Matthew 26:38 (NLT), Jesus instructed Peter, James, and John to "*Stay here and keep watch with Me.*" If you've ever wanted to run from and abandon what you've been given responsibility for, I encourage you to take to heart His call to "Stay here." When the Lord assigns us to a place, He gives us the grace to stay until we've completed our assignment. We can be comforted by the knowledge that He is staying with us *in* it until He releases us *from* it.

If you've ever felt alone in your assignment, know that "He who calls you is faithful, who also will do it" (I Thessalonians 5:24 NKJV). Jesus, who called His disciples into the garden to stay and keep watch with Him, will come into our garden if we invite Him. He'll help us keep watch over what He's entrusted to us. If we face issues in our assigned place that seem too great to handle, we needn't fret over what to do. Instead, we can partner with God by bringing our needs to Him in prayer.

In the Garden of Gethsemane, Jesus focused on the Father and His will alone. He drank the cup of suffering God ordained to complete His assignment to bring salvation to mankind. His decision to willingly and fully obey the will of the Father brought victory to everyone who would follow Him.

The first Adam, through his disobedience, opened the door for sin and Satan to come into the world. With them came every imaginable and unimaginable evil. The second Adam, Jesus Christ, through His total obedience, *took back the garden.* He restored His followers' ability and authority to govern and reign with Him in prayer in the gardens where we are assigned. We'll develop this concept more fully in a later chapter.

Because of what Jesus accomplished through His obedience and finished work, we can stand in authority and power as shepherds in the fields and keepers of the gardens. He has restored us to a rightful relationship with the Father, enabled us to accomplish His purposes for us, and is "making all things new" (Revelation 21:5).

Equipped for Every Good Work

We are, therefore, "complete, thoroughly equipped for every good work" (2 Timothy 3:17 NKJV). We can live this out by modeling humility and repentance, praying, and seeking His face. When faced with a challenging situation, we can choose to act in light of what God's Word says instead of what we feel, see, hear, or think.

I've discovered over the years that if I say about myself or my situation what God's Word says about it, it will eventually become what God's Word says about it. Here's an example of how I incorporated this approach:

Many years ago, when I was in PA school and living for a season away from my family, I'd often say, "I am so tired." I realized I was making this statement about myself almost every day. One day, the Lord spoke this question to my heart, *Is saying this about yourself making you feel less tired?* I thought for a moment and realized that continually saying this about myself was actually making me *more* tired—not the outcome I desired or needed. The Lord then prompted me to say these Scriptures about myself instead:

I am strong in the Lord and in the power of His might (Ephesians 6:10 NKJV).

I can do all things through Christ who strengthens me (Philippians 4:13 NKJV).

Making these daily, truth-filled declarations of God's Word dramatically changed my paradigm regarding the power of His Word. It had power not only because it was *in* me, but as it came *out* of me through the words I speak. I began to experience the truth of these Scriptures and their power to transform me by renewing my mind (Romans 12:2).

Jesus modeled how to respond to circumstances with the truth of God's Word in Matthew 4 as He was tempted by Satan in the wilderness. He responded to every situation Satan threw at Him by speaking God's Word. His example demonstrates that facts change, but the *truth* of God's Word *stands firm* and is *unchangeable*.

Lastly, we are to walk as sons and daughters of God in our assignments. We accomplish this best when we "let [our] light so shine before men that they may see [our] good works and glorify [our] Father in heaven" (Matthew 5:16 NKJV).

Now that we've laid the foundation for the shepherding approach to ministry, both in the marketplace and in all other aspects of life, we'll look at the qualities we must have to walk it out.

Points to Ponder:

1. Where is Jesus calling you to stay and keep watch with Him?

2. What issues would you like to run from?

3. Based on your understanding of Revelation 13:8, what does Jesus' willingness to pay for the sins of the world before they were ever committed mean to you personally?

4. How can you walk in and manifest the victory that Jesus' obedience in the Garden of Gethsemane secured for you?

CHAPTER 4
What It Takes to Shepherd Part I

NOW THAT YOU UNDERSTAND the biblical basis and calling for Christians to shepherd our flocks, you're pumped and ready to dive in. You're thinking, *Tomorrow will be the first day of the rest of my life,* and, *Things will be different now.* People will be grateful to interact with you and dutifully follow wherever you lead because you're there to shepherd them, right? Not necessarily.

This divine interplay doesn't happen at our place of employment or other areas of influence simply because we're believers. We may come to work every day with a big "S" (which stands for *Saint*) printed on our undergarments, but it will take more than this to make an impact in our field. We must earn the right to speak and to be heard. This requires time, patience, and the stuff known as character—with a capital C.

We must never underestimate the value of a solid character. To be solid, it *must* be built according to the Wise Master Builder's plan. God knows what it takes to build us because He *finished* us before He *began* us. His plans always start with the end in mind.

We see this truth underscored in Revelation 13:8 (NKJV), which contains one of the most beloved references to Jesus.

He's called the "Lamb slain from the foundation of the world." Before Adam, before you, or before I could sin, the decision was made and finalized for Jesus to pay the ultimate price for every sin ever committed so we could be reconciled to and in right relationship with God the Father.

God's Good Work in Us

Once we've accepted Jesus as our Savior, God begins the good work of making us more like Jesus every day. Philippians 1:6 (NKJV) says, "being confident of this very thing, that He who has begun a good work in you will complete it until the day of Jesus Christ." Then He lays out His design for character building in 2 Peter 1:5-7 (NKJV): "But also for this very reason, giving all diligence, add to your faith virtue, to virtue knowledge, to knowledge self-control, to self-control persever-ance, to perseverance godliness, to godliness brotherly kindness, and to brotherly kindness love."

These verses illustrate the pattern we're to follow to develop His character in us. The Christian life is more than just placing our faith in Jesus. So many believers stop here. Without question, faith in Jesus is essential to having a relationship with the Father, but He never intended for us to stop at faith. To do so is like walking through a door into a building and remaining in the foyer. Faith is just the threshold to a relationship with God. There's so much more.

Scripture's Character-building Blueprint

Peter lays out the blueprint for our character building in 2 Peter 1:5-7. Let's see what the building holds. There's so much spiritual meat to chew on in these verses that we'll take the next three chapters to digest it all. *Bon Appetit!*

Laying the Framework of Diligence

Peter makes it clear that *diligence* impacts every aspect of our character. Like the framework undergirds a building, diligence supports the other character traits. Peter uses the Greek word *spoudē* because its meaning includes the idea of "haste and earnestness in accomplishing anything."[1]

Sadly, diligence is a rare quality in today's culture. How often have you gone into a business establishment (especially when you're in a hurry) needing a good or service, only to find the one serving you is in no hurry. This is especially true if they work for an hourly wage. Because they earn the same amount per hour whether they provide prompt or slow service, they have little motivation to work hard. In the Kingdom of God, however, our work ethic must be characterized by diligence, especially if we want to have a voice in our field.

The book of Proverbs often speaks about diligence. I've committed several verses to memory. Proverbs 12:24 is one of my favorites and is a core verse for my life: "The hand of the diligent will rule, but the slack hand will be put to forced labor." If we ever hope to lead, we must work with diligence.

Building on the Foundation of Faith

If diligence represents the framework of a building, then *faith* is its foundation. The Greek word Peter uses here is *pistis,* which is defined as the "conviction of the truth of anything, belief."[2] It comes from the root word, *peithō,* which means "to persuade; to induce one by words to believe; to be induced to believe."[3]

The Apostle Paul used this same word in 2 Timothy 1:12 when he wrote, "For I know in whom I have believed and am persuaded" (*peithō*). He also uses this word in Philippians 1:6, "being confident (*peithō*) of this very thing, that He who has begun a good work in you will complete it until the day of Jesus Christ." To earn the right to lead, one must know, be fully persuaded, and walk in confidence about what they believe.

The Character-building Block of Virtue

Now that we've laid the foundation of faith, the first building block we set in place is *virtue,* which Peter described using the Greek word *aretē.* Linguists define this word as "a virtuous course of thought, feeling and action; moral good-ness/excellence."[4] It comes from the root word, a*irō,* which means, "to raise up, elevate, lift up."[5] People who have virtue are worthy of being focused upon. When confronted with difficult people or situations, they don't stoop to lower their standards. They seek to raise others and situations up. They leave a place or environment in a better or elevated condition than they found it.

Here are a few verses that illustrate this character quality of virtue:

- Proverbs 11:11 (italics mine) – "By *the blessing of the upright* a city is *exalted,* but by the mouth of the wicked it is torn down."

- Proverbs 22:3 (italics mine) – "The prudent *sees the evil and hides himself*, but the naive go on, and are punished for it."
- Ephesians 4:29 (italics mine) – "Let no unwholesome word proceed from your mouth, but only such *a word* as is *good for edification* according to the need of the moment, so that it *will give grace* to those who hear."

If you're not sure what's right or wrong in a situation, here's a virtuous approach to take: ask for input from an older, wiser, and more mature believer.

The Character-building Block of Knowledge

It is upon a layer of virtue that we can place the next building block, *knowledge.* In this passage, Peter uses the Greek word *gnōsis*, which is defined as "the act of knowing." It can also mean a "deeper, more perfect, and enlarged knowledge of this religion, such as belongs to the advanced."[6] Merriam-Webster's online dictionary defines knowledge as "the fact or condition of knowing something with familiarity gained through experience or association."[7] To obtain knowledge of any subject, we must spend time studying that subject.

How can we obtain this "deeper more perfect and enlarged knowledge of this religion, such as belongs to the advanced"? By studying God's Word regularly. To lead as a shepherd in our field, we not only have a responsibility, we also have a mandate to study God's Word. The apostle Paul underscores this in the following verses:

2 Timothy 2:15 (KJV) – "Study to shew thyself approved unto God, a workman that needeth not to be ashamed, rightly dividing the word of truth."

It's interesting to note that the origin of the word *study* used in this verse is the same Greek word for "diligence"— *spoudē*. We can't get away from the framework of diligence.

Colossians 3:16 (NKJV) – "Let the word of Christ dwell in you richly in all wisdom, teaching and admonishing one another in psalms and hymns and spiritual songs, singing with grace in your hearts to the Lord."

I learned a lesson many years ago about the value of acquiring knowledge through diligent pursuit. At the time, I was a young wife and mother. Our family had moved to a small town in the Upstate of South Carolina and become part of a church plant. The pastors, Tommy and Barbara Wade, were an older couple I viewed as a spiritual father and mother. They and their two daughters had walked faithfully with the Lord for many years.

Before we moved there, we often visited and stayed in their home. I noticed that whenever I spent time with them, I wanted to pray more, read the Word more, and love Jesus more. Their love for the Lord inspired me to pursue Jesus.

One day, years later when we were all living in the same town, I whined and complained to the Lord about how I didn't know the Word, pray as passionately, or teach the Bible as powerfully as this couple and their daughters did. I felt like God was favoring them and overlooking me.

When I finally quit "bellyaching" (a Southern term used to describe extreme whiny complaining) about my inadequacies, the Lord gently and without condemnation spoke these words to me: "If you want what they have, then do what they do." I remembered their daily rhythm of spending time with Jesus and how they made reading His Word and talking with Him in prayer a priority. I realized I was the only one limiting me. This revelation changed everything.

Points to Ponder:

1. What are some tangible ways the Lord desires to implement or increase the presence of diligence in your character?

2. Think of people in your life that you would describe as virtuous. What is it about them that causes you to view them that way?

3. Do you leave situations and people better or worse than you found them?

4. Do you make spending time with the Lord, reading and studying His Word, and praying a daily priority?

CHAPTER 5
What It Takes to Shepherd Part II

BEFORE WE EXAMINE several more building blocks of character, let's review our text from 2 Peter 1:5-7 (NKJV): "But also for this very reason, giving all diligence, add to your faith virtue, to virtue knowledge, to knowledge self-control, to self-control perseverance, to perseverance godliness, to godliness brotherly kindness, and to brotherly kindness love."

The Character-building Block of Self-control
As we follow the order given in this character-building blueprint, the next component is *self-control*. In this text, the Apostle Peter uses the Greek word *egkrateia*. According to *Strong's Concordance*, one of the biblical uses of this word includes "the virtue of one who masters his desires and passions, especially sensual appetites."[1]

Proverbs 16:32 (italics mine) also powerfully illustrates the value of self-control when it states, "He who is slow to anger is better than the mighty, and he who *rules his spirit* than he who captures a city." The Hebrew word for "rules" in this verse is *mashal*. It is a primitive root word that means "to have dominion or reign."[2] Clearly the writer communicates that one who has reign or dominion over their spirit exhibits greater power than one who can capture a city. That's a lot of power.

To underscore the value of self-control, the apostle Paul lists it as a fruit of the Spirit in Galatians 5:22-23. Scripture is clear—to have a recognized voice as a shepherd in our field, we must exercise self-control.

The Character-building Block of Perseverance

Our next character-building block is *perseverance*. Peter uses the word, *hypomonē*, which Strong defines as, "cheerful (or hopeful) endurance, constancy; patience, patient continuance (waiting)."[3] Notice that the word "patience" is included in this definition. It's also a fruit of the Spirit listed in Galatians 5:22-23. Everyone wants this fruit present in their character, but no one wants to endure the process of developing it.

The root word for *hypomonē* is the Greek word, *hypomenō*. This is a compound word made up of the preposition, *hypo*, which means, "under,"[4] and the verb *menō*, defined as "to stay (in a given place, state, relation or expectancy)."[5] The message conveyed by *hypomenō* is "to stay under (behind), i.e., remain; figuratively, to undergo, i.e., bear (trials)."[6]

I like to define perseverance as *"stick-to-it-iveness."* Larry Pierce in *The Outline of Biblical Usage* presents this word in the New Testament as "the characteristic of a man who is not swerved from his deliberate purpose and his loyalty to faith and piety by even the greatest trials and sufferings."

Jesus demonstrated the greatest example of lifelong perseverance. We can see it portrayed in Luke 9:51 (NKJV), which states that Jesus "steadfastly set His face to go to Jerusalem." The New American Standard Bible translates this verse as, "He was determined to go to Jerusalem." This most certainly illustrates "the characteristic of a man who is not swerved from his deliberate purpose."[7]

Being a shepherd in our field is not for wimps. There are times when we want to give up and walk away. We may even have justifiable reasons. Regardless, we can take heart and maintain our hope if we view our circumstances through the lens of Isaiah 50:7 (NIV), "Because the Sovereign Lord helps me, I will not be disgraced. Therefore have I set my face like flint, and I know I will not be put to shame."

First Thessalonians 5:24 reminds us of God's trustworthiness: "He who calls you is faithful, who also will do it."

Because we are also His sheep, the Good Shepherd watches over us.

Points to Ponder:

1. Why do you think having self-control makes you more powerful than one who has the ability to conquer a city?

2. Why is self-control a crucial character quality? In what areas do you need more self-control?

3. Why is perseverance, the ability to wait hopefully, so necessary for shepherds in their fields?

4. Have you ever felt like giving up and walking away from your assignment? What were the contributing factors in that struggle?

5. How does knowing that the Lord Himself will help you so you won't be disgraced give you the ability to persevere under difficult circumstances?

CHAPTER 6
What It Takes to Shepherd Part III

The Character-building Block of Godliness

As we continue the process of character building as shepherds in the fields, the next layer we need is *godliness*. Peter uses the Greek word *eusebeia*, defined as "piety and holiness," in his list of character traits in 2 Peter 1:5-7. Godliness reflects a "reverence and respect (piety) toward God and the things of God."[1]

In my years of walking with the Lord, I've seen people treat God in one of two ways. Some treat Him as if He's unapproachable and mustn't be bothered with our little problems. He's Almighty God who sits in the heavens. He's not our personal genie in a bottle.

Others treat Jesus like He's their home boy, their bro, their homie. They're so familiar with Him that they forget that He is God, King of Kings, Creator, and Ruler of the universe.

Both these approaches are not only extreme, but erroneous. The Lord is oh-so-approachable, *but* we must follow biblical protocol when we come into His presence and represent Him to others. The proper approach includes demonstrating great reverence for Him because of Who He is, maintaining a heart of thanksgiving as we remember what He has done for us, and understanding that He loves us and wants to be our Provider. When we position ourselves humbly before Him, we're less likely to dishonor Him in our speech or actions. Those in our field desperately need shepherds modeling this behavior of godliness.

The Mortar between the Stones

The final two character-building blocks act as the mortar between the stones of the building and should be slathered generously between every layer. This mortar compound includes *brotherly kindness* and *love*. Because each beautifully compliments the other, we frequently see them operating together.

Let's examine the quality of *brotherly kindness*. The Apostle Peter uses the Greek word, *philadelphia* to describe this trait. Yes, just like the city in Pennsylvania that's known as "The City of Brotherly Love."

Strong's Concordance defines *philadelphia* as the "love of the brethren." Its biblical use conveys not only the love between blood born brothers and sisters, but also includes the love and affection shown by New Testament believers toward each other.[2] This is illustrated in the directives given in Ephesians 4:32, "And be kind to one another, tenderhearted, forgiving one another, even as God in Christ forgave you." Imagine how the world could be turned right side up if we as believers walked in this kind of relationship with each other.

The Most Important Component

The final layer of character building involves the most important component—*love*. Let's look at how love, as referenced in 2 Peter 1:7, is communicated. The Greek word used here is *agape*. It's defined as "affection or benevolence; specifically (plural) a love-feast." This word for love is used 117 times in 106 verses in the Greek concordance of the King James Version[3] and is used in to refer to God's love for us. We can see a derivation used in one of the most well-known and beloved verses in the Bible, John 3:16, "For God so loved (*agapaō*)[4] the world, that He gave His only begotten Son, that whoever believes in Him shall not perish, but have eternal life.

Agape is an unselfish love. It is a love-*feast*, not a snack or a plate of hors d'oeuvres. It always puts the best interests of the object of this love before the one giving the love. It exemplifies the love of God Himself, as seen in I John 4:16, "We have come to know and have believed the love which God has for us. *God is love*, and the one who abides in love abides in God, and God abides in him."

Agape love, the love that motivates God's actions, is what our character should be wrapped in, much like the exterior of a building. Everything visible to those in our field—our words and our actions—should convey God's love and character.

As we conclude these three chapters on the discussion of character building, I can't end more powerfully than the author does in 2 Peter 1:8-10: "For if these things are yours and abound, you will be neither barren nor unfruitful in the knowledge of our Lord Jesus Christ. For he who lacks these things is shortsighted, even to blindness, and has forgotten that he was cleansed from his old sins. Therefore, brethren, be even more diligent to make your call and election sure, for if you do these things you will never stumble."

Selfless Love
Brotherly kindness

Godliness

Patience/Perseverance

Self-control

Knowledge

Virtue

FAITH

Points to Ponder:

1. In your experience, which perception of the Lord bests reflects your approach to Him—unapproachable or too familiar?

2. What danger(s) is/are there in both approaches?

3. Do the directives in Ephesians 4:32 challenge you? In what ways?

4. How has the Lord displayed His "love feast" to you? How can you practically display it to those in your field?

CHAPTER 7
Divine Insight to Deal with People and Problems

HOW MANY TIMES HAVE YOU HEARD someone say, "My _____ *(job, ministry, life)* would be great if I just didn't have to deal with people!" People are part of every aspect of our life. We can't live without them, and sometimes, we can't live *with* them! We can't minister in our field without interacting with others, and some people can be difficult. Having wise insight into how best to deal with challenging people is an invaluable tool. Fortunately, God loves everyone and desires to help us live together in a way that honors Him and each other.

God's Word contains much wisdom about how to interact with people in challenging circumstances while maintaining a good testimony. In this chapter we'll focus on how to deal with serious problems with potentially devastating outcomes. When we face a crisis of magnitude, we desperately need God's direction to walk through it to recovery. Fortunately, John 2 provides guidance for how to walk through a challenging situation wisely and righteously.

Ancient Wisdom with Modern Application
John begins the second chapter of his gospel by describing events that took place during a wedding in the city of Cana. In

the culture of the day, the bridegroom's family was responsible for providing all the food and wine for the feast that followed the ceremony. Because wedding events in the first century would sometimes last up to a week, this involved a considerable financial commitment. In John 2:1-12, we read that on the third day, the wine ran out. This may not sound like a big deal, but in that culture, such a crisis would have caused great disgrace for the bridegroom's family. Somehow Mary, the mother of Jesus, became aware of the problem. Let's see how she handled the situation and gain wisdom from her response.

The Importance of Keeping Confidences

As soon as Mary discovered the problem, she brought it to Jesus' attention. Her action provides us with the most important step in solving a problem, big or small—bring it to Jesus! This is especially true when we become privy to sensitive insight and/or information about a person or problem. The first person you need to speak to isn't your friend, neighbor, or coworker, it's Jesus.

To be a shepherd who gains the confidence of those in our field, we must first demonstrate that we can keep a confidence. We should ask ourselves these questions: Do I know how to keep my mouth closed when I know sensitive information? Am I a source that leaks? Can I be trusted with others' confidences?"

God's Word has much to say about the issue of keeping confidences. Proverbs 11:13 states, "He who goes about as a talebearer reveals secrets, but he who is trustworthy conceals a matter." The word "trustworthy" comes from two Hebrew words, *aman*, from which the Hebrew word for "truth" is derived,[1] and *ruwach* which is translated "spirit."[2] Together, these two words convey the image of one who is "faithful of spirit."[3] I want to be known as one who is full of truth, and who can faithfully keep and steward well the confidence of others. I suspect you do, too.

It's tempting to share a juicy morsel of information with others, especially in a group. Proverbs 10:19 (NLT) addresses this by saying, "Too much talk leads to sin. Be sensible and keep your mouth shut." This verse warns me that the pleasure of gossiping isn't worth the pain it might inflict on the one being discussed. No amount of temporary gratification will outweigh the damage that comes from betraying another and losing their trust.

Proverbs 18:8 (KJV) provides another warning about gossip: "The words of a talebearer are as wounds, and they go down into the innermost parts of the belly." This passage doesn't tell us who's being wounded. Is it the bearer of the tales, the recipient of the tale bearing, or the subject of the tale? Regardless, the effects of gossiping go "down into the innermost parts of the belly," making it difficult to forget what you've heard and negatively skewing the way you view someone. Any way you look at it, it's unwise to be involved in gossip.

Now that we've established that keeping a confidence is a key to shepherding with integrity, let's return to the passages in John 2 and study Mary's approach to the problem of no wine.

Perseverance and Persistence

She could have been dissuaded or discouraged by Jesus' initial response to her. However, she modeled perseverance and

persistence. (Remember the building blocks of a solid character?) She demonstrated leadership by saying to those serving at
the wedding feast, "Whatever He says to you, do it" (v. 5).

I can think of no greater message to communicate to those
whom I shepherd than to encourage absolute obedience to
Jesus. I can do this not only with my words, but with my
actions—how I obey Jesus. This is paramount because we never
know who's watching and listening to our example.

When we read this account to completion, we see how
Mary's instruction to the servants inspired their obedience and
prepared the way for a miraculous outcome. Jesus exercised His
divine power and transformed the jars of water into fine wine.
The bridegroom's family was spared, and Jesus performed His
first public miracle.

As shepherds in the field, we're called not only to watch
over and protect, but to provide instruction in righteousness.
When we do, God uses us to help others, like the servants in
this account, to witness the miraculous. You never know how
your words and manner of conduct can connect others to
supernatural power. God desires this to be our lifestyle.

Dealing with Offenses

Another important tool to help you deal with people and
problems that arise in your field is wisdom from the Lord,
specifically regarding how to deal with offenses. If Jesus, in
Luke 17:1 (NKJV), felt it important enough to mention that
offenses will come, then I'd be remiss if I didn't discuss how to
biblically address them. Before we delve into the particulars,
let's read the verse.

"Then He said to the disciples, 'It is impossible that no offenses should come, but woe to him through whom they do come!'"

It's interesting to note that the Greek word Jesus used for "offenses" in this passage is *skandalon*. It's the word from which "scandal" is derived. It means an "occasion to fall (of stumbling), thing that offends, stumbling block."[4] It speaks of an issue you feel like you just can't get past or over. Every time you try to move forward, you trip over the issue.

Let's look at the wisdom Jesus gives us to deal with troubling scenarios in Matthew 18:15-16 (NKJV). He states, "Moreover if your brother sins against you, go and tell him his fault between you and him alone. If he hears you, you have gained your brother. But if he will not hear, take with you one or two more, that 'by the mouth of two or three witnesses every word may be established.'"

Jesus' instruction reminds us that, if possible, private matters should remain private. If it's safe to do so, talk with the other person alone. We shouldn't seek an audience with or involve others and share our grievances about a person or situation before we speak with the offending person. These actions characterize the "talebearer" mentioned earlier, not the peacemaker. Such an approach is unwise.

When we meet with the person who has offended, our goal should be to confront them in love and bring about a righteous outcome – not to crush or humiliate them. We must determine our goal before confronting. Ask, "What do I hope to accomplish?" When you meet, stick to the issue. Don't get sidetracked. Staying on topic helps keep the focus on being reconciled, not to conquer the other person.

If you're unable to accomplish the mission with a private meeting, take a trusted, mature, wise witness with you. They should be someone who has demonstrated that they walk in a righteous, Christ-like manner. James 3:18 gives a glimpse of this type of character: "And the seed whose fruit is righteousness is sown in peace by those who make peace."

We can't resolve all conflicts, but if we avoid gossip, follow biblical guidelines for conflict resolution, and seek to love and restore others, we can be successful peacemakers among those God has called us to shepherd.

Points to Ponder:

1. Is there someone you interact with on a regular basis that challenges your ability to walk in a Christ-like manner?

2. Who is the *first* person you usually speak with about problems or difficult people?

3. How can you incorporate Mary's example of bringing problems to Jesus first in every field in which you function as a shepherd, including your home, neighborhood, work, church, or other place you frequent?

4. Who do you consider a trusted, mature, wise witness who has demonstrated that they walk in a righteous, Christ-like manner with others? Can this be said of you? If not, why? What must you do to correct this?

CHAPTER 8

Releasing the Voice of God and Changing the Atmosphere

WE SEE IN Genesis 1:1-31 how God created everything except man and woman by His *words*. Let's set the stage for contextual purpose by examining verse 2:

"The earth was formless and void, and darkness was over the surface of the deep, and the Spirit of God was moving over the surface of the waters."

This verse is packed with important words that paint a graphic picture of the condition of the earth when "the Spirit of God was moving over the face of the waters." Some theologians believe something catastrophic occurred between verses 1 and 2. Time and space won't allow for further study into this possibility, but you may want to dig a little deeper on your own.

Let's break this verse apart into the main Hebrew words and their definitions to give insight into the condition of creation:

- *Tohuw* is translated as "without form" or "formless," and is defined as "to lie waste; a desolation, desert; a worthless thing; confusion, empty place."[1]
- *Bohuw* is translated as "void," and is defined as, "a vacuity; and undistinguishable ruin."[2]

- *Choshek* is translated as "darkness," and is defined as "(literally) darkness; figuratively as misery, destruction, death, ignorance, sorrow, wickedness."[3]

- *Paniym* is translated as "surface," and is defined as "the face (as the part that turns)."[4]

- *Těhowm* is translated as "deep," and is defined as "an abyss (as a surging mass of water)."[5] Larry Pierce, in his study tool, *The Outline of Biblical Usage,* includes the words "sea" and "the grave"[6] as synonyms for *těhowm.* It is derived from the Hebrew root word, *huwm,* which is defined as "to make an uproar, or agitate greatly."[7]

- *Ruwach* is translated "Spirit." This word is used in the Bible when speaking of the "wind, breath, mind, spirit" of God and man[8] It is also used with respect to the breath of animals in the account of the flood seen in Genesis 7:15, "So they went into the ark to Noah, by twos of all flesh in which was the *breath* of life."

- *Elohiym* is translated as "the supreme God." He is both the supreme ruler and judge.[9]

- *Rachaph* is translated as "moving," and is defined as "to brood: to flutter, move, shake."[10] This is the picture of a mother hen as she broods over her nest. The *Gesenius' Hebrew-Chaldee Lexicon* has this to say about the word "rachaph": "To be moved, affected with the feeling of tender love, hence to cherish" much like an eagle cherishes its young.[11]

Rewriting Genesis 1:2 in My Own Words

Often, when studying God's Word, I rewrite the verse in my own words by breaking a verse apart into its individual original words. This gives me a clearer, more vivid illustration of it. Here's how I rewrote Genesis 1:2:

> The earth was a desolate, worthless, and undistinguishable wasteland that created a vacuum full of confusion, darkness, ignorance, sorrow, wickedness, misery, destruction, and death. It was a grave that contained nothing but deep, dark hopelessness. Its atmosphere was consumed with an uproarious sound of agitation... but then... *the Spirit of the Supreme God,* Who was moved with great affection and tender love for His creation, brooded over it, like a mother hen, and released His breath in the face of this hopelessness.

Genesis 1:3 states, "Then God said, 'Let there be light'; and there was light." The word *amar* is the most frequently used Hebrew word translated as a form of the verb "to say." In the study tool, *The Outline of Biblical Usage,* Larry Pierce includes the following examples of how this word can be translated: "to say, to answer, to say in one's heart, to think, to command, to promise, to intend."[12]

It's also worth mentioning that this is the first reference in Scripture of God's voice. Christian teacher, author, and speaker, R.T. Kendall defines the term, "the law of first mention," as, "the way a word is first used in the Bible will be the way this word is largely understood thereafter."[13] Therefore, we can forever see the connection between the voice of God and the release of power, especially *creative power.*

Scripture declares all creation is to reflect God the Creator. Of His creation, humans are the only ones who are like Him in that we can "think, intend, answer, command, and promise."[14] No other creature has been given this incredible ability, privilege, and responsibility. As Jesus said in Luke 12:48 (NLT), "When someone has been given much, much will be required in return; and when someone has been entrusted with much, even more will be required."

Also in Genesis 1:3, we see the connection between the voice of God and the presence of light. It's apparent God places a high priority on light. To demonstrate this truth, let's look at two passages that underscore this:

- John 1:4 – "In Him was life, and the life was the *light* of men."
- I John 1:5 – "This is the message which we have heard from Him and declare to you, that God is *light* and in Him is *no darkness at all.*"

How Does This Impact Us as Shepherds in the Fields?

To answer this, let's go back to Genesis 1:26 and look at God's intention as He formed man:

"Then God said, 'Let Us make man in *Our image*, according to Our *likeness*'" (italics mine).

The word "image" is the Hebrew word, *tselem,* which meaning includes the word, "resemblance."[15] Have you ever said, "You sure do resemble your father"? What we mean is that there's something, either in the way someone looks or behaves, that makes us think of their father. This same concept can be applied to mankind. Because we are made in God's image, those who see us should think of our Heavenly Father because we resemble Him so much. What a privilege—and a responsibility—to be image bearers of God!

Additionally, we see we were created according to His *likeness*. The Hebrew word for "likeness" is *demuwth*. It's also defined as, "resemblance."[16] Why would God use two different words to communicate the same concept? According to author, internationally recognized Christian apologist, and speaker, Don Stewart, "This is an example of a common device in Hebrew literature known as parallelism. The two words are synonymous. The Hebrews would often emphasize something by stating the same thing in two different ways. This seems to be what we have here. There is no real difference between image and likeness."[17]

In the midst of confusion, darkness, and death, God's voice is the instrument that brings order, light, and life. As believers and followers of Jesus, we have the Spirit of God, the same Spirit that raised Jesus from the dead living inside us (Romans 8:11).

Colossians 3:16 states we are called to "let the *word of Christ* richly dwell within you." Not only are we created in His image and according to His likeness, but we also have the Spirit of God and the Word of God dwelling within us. We possess the "voice" of God within us.

But God doesn't just want to have His voice inside us, He wants us to *release* His voice into our environment and circumstances just like He would.

In 2 Corinthians 5:20, the Apostle Paul introduces the concept of believers being "ambassadors for Christ." As ambassadors, I can think of no better way to represent Jesus and His Kingdom on earth than as a shepherd releasing His voice, which incorporates His Spirit and His Word, into the lives and atmospheres within our fields.

Without the presence of God, people and environments are full of confusion, darkness, despair, hopelessness, and death. They're like graves filled with the sounds of roaring and agitation. This is why we must walk as a shepherd and bring the peace, order, light, hope, and life that accompanies the releasing of His voice, heard within ours, into our field.

Let's conclude with a portion of Scripture that beautifully illustrates the precious effect of a shepherd's voice, John 10:2-4 (NKJV):

"But he who enters by the door is the shepherd of the sheep. To him the doorkeeper opens, and the sheep hear his voice; and he calls his own sheep by name and leads them out. And when he brings out his own sheep, he goes before them; and the sheep follow him, for they know his voice."

This passage refers to Jesus as the True Shepherd. It gives us tremendous insight into the love of the Lord toward the sheep He knows intimately and calls by name. It also provides us with a priceless model to follow as shepherds, demonstrating the value of releasing the gentleness and intimacy of His voice by how we communicate with those in our field.

Points to Ponder:

1. What descriptive words would you use to illustrate the picture of creation in Genesis 1:2?

2. How did God respond to the apparently hopeless situation of His creation?

3. Can you think of circumstances, situations, and relationships that affect you or are affected by you that can benefit from the voice of God (His Word and His Spirit inside you) being released by you?

4. Write out a personalized statement that includes what His Word says about your situation. Read it aloud as a prayer.

CHAPTER 9
Identifying with the Shepherds

WHEN YOU WATCH A MOVIE or read a book, do you find yourself identifying with one of the characters? I don't know about you, but I always identify with and pull for the underdog. When Rocky Balboa, against all odds, landed the knockout punch to Apollo Creed in the 1976 iconic film, *Rocky*, everyone, especially me, cheered.

The tenacity of Sally Field's Academy Award winning character, Edna Spalding, in the movie, *Places in the Heart* continues to inspire me. I'll never forget the scene when Edna, with bloodied fingers, continues to pick cotton into the night to make the sale on time, so she can save the family farm and keep her children.

Human nature connects us with others when we find something familiar or unifying in their story. Thankfully, we're not limited to movie screen characters to inspire us. Here are a few real examples of people living as shepherds in their fields.

Ruth

A couple of years ago Ruth and her husband, John, relocated to the South from the Midwest, where they had spent their entire lives. It was a real step of faith for these fifty-somethings to uproot and move across the country, but they did it.

Ruth is a soft-spoken, gentle-spirited woman who recognizes that everywhere she goes is her field. She's been gifted with a Holy Spirit-led sensitivity to the needs of those with whom she comes in contact.

This gift has been especially helpful in her field as an Interior Designer in a furniture store. She frequently prays for and with her clients and looks for ways to bring the presence of Jesus into her workplace. But it hasn't always been easy.

"For the entire first year in my workplace, no one returned my 'Good Morning!' or even spoke to me," Ruth remembers. "I was brand new to the area and had no friends. Because I'm very relational, I found this especially painful."

But through her patience and perseverance, the atmosphere in her workplace changed. "Now, I get a 'Good Morning' in return each day," she says with a satisfied smile.

What made her stick it out when others would have left? "God assigned me to this place," Ruth said with tears in her eyes, "and when I'm no longer here, I want them to be impressed with Jesus' love for them." A key verse that has helped her during this season has been Hosea 10:12, "Sow with a view to righteousness, reap in accordance with kindness; break up your fallow ground, for it is time to seek the LORD until He comes to rain righteousness on you."

Denise

Denise has the privilege of watching over a flock of neighbors and friends. Her great heart of love and compassion grew out of painful experience. She and her husband, Lee, recently moved back to their beloved region after living for a few years in what Denise describes as "an emotional desert." She had a beautiful home on a lake but felt completely isolated. She missed the community she had once known and felt like she was dying on the vine.

As soon as she received word that she and Lee were returning home, Denise committed to shepherd those around her in whatever neighborhood the Lord placed them. She jumped into this with both feet, inviting four different neighbors to her home for brunch within weeks of moving in. Remembering how lonely she had felt, she figured others within her sphere of influence might feel the same. She often delivers homemade bread when a new neighbor moves in and sends meals to those who are sick.

As a breast cancer survivor, Denise also knows what it's like to walk through illness. Her journey has opened the door for her to show the love of God to others who have been affected by sickness or disease. She shepherds her flock through phone calls or texts, homecooked meals, and handwritten cards. She often shares a devotional book that ministered to her during her season of illness.

Denise has beautifully illustrated 2 Corinthians 1:3-4, "Blessed be the God and Father of our Lord Jesus Christ, the Father of mercies and God of all comfort, who comforts us in all our affliction *so that we will be able to comfort those who are in any affliction with the comfort with which we ourselves are comforted by God* [italics mine]." This precious woman is one of my dearest and most cherished friends, and I have often benefitted from being one of the sheep in her field.

Denise wants to be remembered as one who "loved well, followed her Savior's example, was there with a heart of compassion, and always pointed others to Christ." She hopes others will follow her example of seeing and reaching out to others, especially their neighbors, as a shepherd to a flock.

Pete

Pete, a self-described "heathern" (a very southern pronunciation of the word, "heathen," one who does not know God and therefore lives in an unrighteous manner), grew up on what he calls, "the mill hill" in a small Southern town in the first half of the 20th century. In his early years, he considered himself an agnostic, someone who is unsure of the existence of God.

He married Barbara, his high school sweetheart, and they lived much like their parents had. They worked hard, struggled to make ends meet, and lived without a relationship with Christ.

Then, on a divinely orchestrated day in 1974, at the age of 38, Pete met Jesus. Barbara had also recently repented, returning to her Savior after walking away from her faith many years prior.

Pete had worked for many years as a maintenance planner and scheduler at a local manufacturing plant. His co-workers knew him as a man who lived in total opposition to the ways of Christ.

In the weeks and months following his conversion, they saw God radically transform his life by the power of the gospel. Someone who was once "dead in his trespasses and sins" become *alive* after encountering the resurrected Savior.

Pete dedicated his life to sharing his testimony verbally as well as through his lifestyle, especially to the sheep in his field. He fervently prayed for his fellow employees in the years before he retired. As a shepherd, he created opportunities to introduce his co-workers to the Lord.

He often shared the Word of God in casual conversation. He'd talk about a nugget of spiritual truth he'd mined during his personal devotion time or share insight he'd received in the prayer meetings and Bible Studies he conducted in his office during break times. Many of his co-workers were born again and delivered out of the kingdom of darkness because he shepherded while working as a plant maintenance supervisor.

Now, years later, Pete has experienced the truth of Isaiah 55:11, "So will My word be which goes forth from My mouth; It will not return to Me empty, without accomplishing what I desire, and without succeeding in the matter for which I sent it." He knows he deposited something eternal in the lives of others.

I'm one of those fortunate to have been shepherded by Pete. One of my greatest takeaways from Pete's ministry is a statement he often makes: "Nothing and *no one* satisfies like Jesus."

So true Pete. So very true.

Dale

Dale functions as a wonderful example of a shepherd in the field while serving as a licensed professional counselor at a high school. He views the students, faculty, and school staff as the sheep of his pasture.

A personality profile revealed, in addition to being in a helping profession, that Dale also has a helper personality. But this isn't what gives Dale his edge. His belief in and commitment to Jesus, along with the insight he gained as a pastor has equipped him well to shepherd his particular flock. Incorporating the heart and vision of a shepherd with the training and perspective as a pastor and therapist help him care for the whole person.

Dale doesn't just assess the mental and emotional health of his flock. He also looks out for their physical, spiritual, and sometimes domestic needs. He may discover that a student doesn't have food at home or is living without electricity because of an unpaid utility bill. He's helped facilitate alternative housing for students living in unhealthy living arrangements or without a place to live at all. As soon as he discovers a need, he looks for a way to connect that need to available resources.

His greatest contributions, however, are less tangible. He provides a safe place for students to talk about their issues, especially the most personal ones. Then he helps bridge the gap between the students and their teachers. His willingness to listen without judgment has allowed Dale to discover matters of abuse, neglect, and academic challenges. He handles these confidences professionally, but with the perspective of a shepherd who wants the absolute highest and best for his flock. His compassionate approach helps him share insight with the teachers into the personalities of their students and their individual learning styles.

Dale's greatest desire is to positively represent his heavenly Father to his flock—the students, faculty, and school staff—so their view of God is accurate and undistorted. Many of Dale's students have grown up without an earthly father in their lives and homes, so they benefit greatly from seeing what a godly man and father looks like.

Kathy

Kathy shepherds the most precious of all flocks—her children. Against the flow of current culture, she's chosen to be a shepherd in the field of homemaking and stay-at-home motherhood, much like her mother and grandmother before her. Making ends meet is challenging most months, but Kathy and her husband, Ben, partner well with each other to live within their means. They strive to model faithfulness in stewarding their finances. Everything they do reflects their individual relationship with Christ and the priority they place on making Him Lord of their marriage and their home.

Kathy's children learn the Word of God through what she speaks and how she lives her life as an example before them. They've seen her demonstrate the character quality of faithfulness, not only in the home and with her family, but also toward her parents and friends. As busy as life can be for a young mother of small children, Kathy still nurtures the relationship with her aging parents by calling and checking on them regularly.

Like her role model, the Proverbs 31 woman, she "stretches out her hands to the needy" (v. 20). When her friend was bedridden during her second pregnancy, Kathy brought food and cared for her friend's very active 3-year-old child so she could nap.

She views her home and family as her garden that she must tend and keep. Kathy is acutely aware that time passes quickly. She must seize the opportunities God gives her and capture and savor every moment.

She often ponders the wisdom of her mother's words, "Kathy, there will be plenty of time in the future to make more money, but the time in the home, with your children, to make eternal deposits passes quickly." One of her favorite verses is Proverbs 14:4, and she has modified it to best illustrate her heart for her home and children:

> *Where no children are, the home is clean, but much joy and blessings come by the presence of children.*

In a time when many women, especially young wives and mothers, find their sense of worth in their career and paycheck, like Mary in Luke 10:42, Kathy "has chosen the good portion, which will not be taken away from her." She knows the most precious treasures in her life are her children, and the most noble assignment she currently has is to shepherd them. What a wise and valuable gift she is to her family and the world.

The Heart of the Matter

Shepherds in the fields embody what Jesus meant in John 14:9, when He said, "He who has seen Me has seen the Father." As Ruth, Denise, Pete, Dale, and Kathy serve God where He has placed them, they reveal the Father's great heart of love to the world.

Points to Ponder:

1. With whom do you most identify among these shepherds I've described?
2. Why?
3. Now that you've seen a variety of shepherding approaches, can you identify other shepherds you know?
4. What shepherding qualities do they possess?
5. How can you incorporate a shepherding approach to your field?

CHAPTER 10
What Shepherding Is All About

WE FIND OUR ULTIMATE CALLING as shepherds in the fields in 2 Corinthians 5:18-20:

> Now all things are of God, who has reconciled us to Himself through Jesus Christ, and has given us *the ministry of reconciliation*, that is, that God was in Christ reconciling the world to Himself, not imputing their trespasses to them, and has committed to us the word of reconciliation. Now then, we are ambassadors for Christ, as though God were pleading through us: we implore you on Christ's behalf, be reconciled to God (italics mine).

The Apostle Paul uses the Greek word *katallagē* when speaking of reconciliation. This word is defined as, "exchange, i.e., restoration to (the divine) favor; atonement."[1] It's derived from the Greek root word, *katallassō*, meaning "to change mutually; reconcile."[2] This word in its original language, however, as seen in *Thayer's Greek Lexicon*, conveys the image of "to change, exchange, as coins for others of equal value; hence, to reconcile (those who are at variance)."[3]

Doesn't this beautifully describe our mission as shepherds in the fields? God calls us to be a divine connection between Himself, a loving and Holy God, and a hopelessly lost and sin-filled world. We have the privilege of communicating, with our words and by the example of our lives, what Jesus accomplished for us. It's all about *the great exchange of the sinless Son of a holy God for the sinful sinner!* This most certainly illustrates a reconciliation of "those who are at variance."

No passage more clearly conveys God's heart about being rightly positioned in our field than Romans 10:13-15 (NKJV):

> For whoever calls on the name of the LORD shall be saved. How then shall they call on Him in whom they have not believed? And how shall they believe in Him of whom they have not heard? And how shall they hear without a preacher? And how shall they preach unless they are sent? As it is written: How beautiful are the feet of those who preach the gospel of peace, who bring glad tidings of good things!

It is my great honor to be called to shepherd within my field of medicine. What about you? Are you hearing the calling to be a shepherd in your field? Believers will experience no greater joy than knowing we are in our field of calling fulfilling the purpose for which we were created.

My great desire is that while reading this book, and perhaps using it as a Bible study, you have gained a vision of yourself as a shepherd in whatever field God has assigned you to. May you choose today to embark on the most wonderful and always exciting adventure of discovering His plan for you as a shepherd in the field!

~Susan Wells

Notes

Introduction

1. "field." *Merriam-Webster.com*. Merriam-Webster, 2020. Web. 4 June 2020.

2. Ibid.

3. Ibid.

Chapter 1

1. "G4166 – poimēn – Strong's Greek Lexicon (NASB)." Blue Letter Bible. Web. 04 June, 2020. <https://www.blueletterbible.org//lang/lexicon/lexicon.cfm?Strongs=G4166&t=NASB>.

2. Ibid.

3. "G5442 – phylassō – Strong's Greek Lexicon (NASB)." Blue Letter Bible. Web. 04 June, 2020. <https://www.blueletterbible.org//lang/lexicon/lexicon.cfm?Strongs=G5442&t=NASB>.

4. Ibid.

5. "G5438 – phylakē – Strong's Greek Lexicon (NASB)." Blue Letter Bible. Web. 04 June, 2020. <https://www.blueletterbible.org//lang/lexicon/lexicon.cfm?Strongs=G5438&t=NASB>.

6. Ibid.

7. "G3571 – nyx – Strong's Greek Lexicon (NASB)." Blue Letter Bible. Web. 05 June, 2020. <https://www.blueletterbible.org//lang/lexicon/lexicon.cfm?Strongs=G3571&t=NASB>.

8. Ibid.

9. "field." *Merriam-Webster.com*. Merriam-Webster, 2020. Web. 4 June 2020.

Chapter 2

1. "H3947 – laqach – Strong's Hebrew Lexicon (NASB)." Blue Letter Bible. Web. 05 June, 2020. <https://www.blueletterbible.org//lang/lexicon/lexicon.cfm?Strongs=H3947&t=NASB>.

2. "H5117 – nuwach – Strong's Hebrew Lexicon (NASB)." Blue Letter Bible. Web. 05 June, 2020. <https://www.blueletterbible.org//lang/lexicon/lexicon.cfm?Strongs=H5117&t=NASB>.

3. "H1588 – gan – Strong's Hebrew Lexicon (NASB)." Blue Letter Bible. Web. 05 June, 2020. <https://www.blueletterbible.org//lang/lexicon/lexicon.cfm?Strongs=H1588&t=NASB>.

4. "H1598 – ganan – Strong's Hebrew Lexicon (NASB)." Blue Letter Bible. Web. 05 June, 2020. <https://www.blueletterbible.org//lang/lexicon/lexicon.cfm?Strongs=H1598&t=NASB>.

5. "H5647 – 'abad – Strong's Hebrew Lexicon (NASB)." Blue Letter Bible. Web. 08 June, 2020.

<https://www.blueletterbible.org//lang/lexicon/lexicon.cfm?Strongs=
H5647&t=NASB>.

6. "H8104 – shamar – Strong's Hebrew Lexicon (NASB)." Blue
Letter Bible. Web. 08 June, 2020.
<https://www.blueletterbible.org//lang/lexicon/lexicon.cfm?Strongs=
H8104&t=NASB>.

7. "H5731 – 'Eden – Strong's Hebrew Lexicon (NASB)." Blue Letter
Bible. Web. 08 June, 2020.
<https://www.blueletterbible.org//lang/Lexicon/Lexicon.cfm?Strongs
=H5731&t=NASB>.

8. "H5727 – 'adan – Strong's Hebrew Lexicon (NASB)." Blue Letter
Bible. Web. 08 June, 2020.
<https://www.blueletterbible.org//lang/lexicon/lexicon.cfm?Strongs=
H5727&t=NASB>.

Chapter 4

1. "G4710 – spoudē – Strong's Greek Lexicon (NASB)." Blue Letter
Bible. Web. 09 June, 2020.
<https://www.blueletterbible.org//lang/Lexicon/Lexicon.cfm?Strongs
=G4710&t=NASB>.

2. "G4102 – pistis – Strong's Greek Lexicon (NASB)." Blue Letter
Bible. Web. 09 June, 2020.
<https://www.blueletterbible.org//lang/Lexicon/Lexicon.cfm?Strongs
=G4102&t=NASB>.

3. "G3982 – peithō – Strong's Greek Lexicon (NASB)." Blue Letter
Bible. Web. 09 June, 2020.
<https://www.blueletterbible.org//lang/Lexicon/lexicon.cfm?Strongs
=G3982&t=NASB>.

4. "G703 – aretē – Strong's Greek Lexicon (NASB)." Blue Letter
Bible. Web. 09 June, 2020.
<https://www.blueletterbible.org//lang/Lexicon/Lexicon.cfm?Strongs
=G703&t=NASB>.

5. "G142 – airō – Strong's Greek Lexicon (NASB)." Blue Letter
Bible. Web. 09 June, 2020.
<https://www.blueletterbible.org//lang/Lexicon/lexicon.cfm?Strongs
=G142&t=NASB>.

6. "G1108 – gnōsis – Strong's Greek Lexicon (NASB)." Blue Letter
Bible. Web. 09 June, 2020.
<https://www.blueletterbible.org//lang/Lexicon/Lexicon.cfm?Strongs
=G1108&t=NASB>.

7. "knowledge." *Merriam-Webster.com*. Merriam-Webster, 2020.
Web. 9 June 2020.

Chapter 5

1. "G1466 – egkrateia – Strong's Greek Lexicon (NASB)." Blue
Letter Bible. Web. 10 June, 2020.
<https://www.blueletterbible.org//lang/Lexicon/Lexicon.cfm?Strongs
=G1466&t=NASB>.

2. "H4910 – mashal – Strong's Hebrew Lexicon (NASB)." Blue
Letter Bible. Web. 10 June, 2020.
<https://www.blueletterbible.org//lang/Lexicon/Lexicon.cfm?Strongs
=H4910&t=NASB>.

3. "G5281 – hypomonē – Strong's Greek Lexicon (NASB)." Blue
Letter Bible. Web. 10 June, 2020.
<https://www.blueletterbible.org//lang/Lexicon/Lexicon.cfm?Strongs
=G5281&t=NASB>.

4. "G5259 – hypo – Strong's Greek Lexicon (NASB)." Blue Letter Bible. Web. 10 June, 2020. <https://www.blueletterbible.org//lang/Lexicon/lexicon.cfm?Strongs=G5259&t=NASB>.

5. "G3306 – menō – Strong's Greek Lexicon (NASB)." Blue Letter Bible. Web. 10 June, 2020. <https://www.blueletterbible.org//lang/Lexicon/lexicon.cfm?Strongs=G3306&t=NASB>.

6. "G5278 – hypomenō – Strong's Greek Lexicon (NASB)." Blue Letter Bible. Web. 10 June, 2020. <https://www.blueletterbible.org//lang/Lexicon/lexicon.cfm?Strongs=G5278&t=NASB>.

7. "G5281 – hypomonē – Strong's Greek Lexicon (NASB)." Blue Letter Bible. Web. 10 June, 2020. <https://www.blueletterbible.org//lang/Lexicon/Lexicon.cfm?Strongs=G5281&t=NASB>.

Chapter 6

1. "G2150 – eusebeia – Strong's Greek Lexicon (NASB)." Blue Letter Bible. Web. 11 June, 2020. <https://www.blueletterbible.org//lang/Lexicon/Lexicon.cfm?Strongs=G2150&t=NASB>.

2. "G5360 – philadelphia – Strong's Greek Lexicon (NASB)." Blue Letter Bible. Web. 11 June, 2020. <https://www.blueletterbible.org//lang/Lexicon/Lexicon.cfm?Strongs=G5360&t=NASB>.

3. "G26 – agapē – Strong's Greek Lexicon (NASB)." Blue Letter Bible. Web. 11 June, 2020.

<https://www.blueletterbible.org//lang/Lexicon/Lexicon.cfm?Strongs
=G26&t=NASB>.

4. "G25 – agapaō – Strong's Greek Lexicon (NASB)." Blue Letter
Bible. Web. 11 June, 2020.
<https://www.blueletterbible.org//lang/Lexicon/lexicon.cfm?Strongs
=G25&t=NASB>.

Chapter 7

1. "H539 – 'aman – Strong's Hebrew Lexicon (NASB)." Blue Letter
Bible. Web. 15 June, 2020.
<https://www.blueletterbible.org//lang/Lexicon/Lexicon.cfm?Strongs
=H539&t=NASB>.

2. "H7307 – ruwach – Strong's Hebrew Lexicon (NASB)." Blue
Letter Bible. Web. 15 June, 2020.
<https://www.blueletterbible.org//lang/Lexicon/Lexicon.cfm?Strongs
=H7307&t=NASB>.

3. "Proverbs 11 (NASB) – He who goes about as." Blue Letter Bible.
Web. 15 June, 2020.
<https://www.blueletterbible.org/nasb/pro/11/13/ss1/s_639013>.

4. "G4625 – skandalon – Strong's Greek Lexicon (NASB)." Blue
Letter Bible. Web. 15 June, 2020.
<https://www.blueletterbible.org//lang/lexicon/lexicon.cfm?Strongs=
G4625&t=NASB>.

Chapter 8

1. "H8414 – tohuw – Strong's Hebrew Lexicon (NASB)." Blue Letter
Bible. Web. 16 June, 2020.
<https://www.blueletterbible.org//lang/Lexicon/Lexicon.cfm?Strongs
=H8414&t=NASB>.

2. "H922 – bohuw – Strong's Hebrew Lexicon (NASB)." Blue Letter Bible. Web. 16 June, 2020. <https://www.blueletterbible.org//lang/Lexicon/Lexicon.cfm?Strongs=H922&t=NASB>.

3. "H2822 – choshek – Strong's Hebrew Lexicon (NASB)." Blue Letter Bible. Web. 16 June, 2020. <https://www.blueletterbible.org//lang/Lexicon/Lexicon.cfm?Strongs=H2822&t=NASB>.

4. "H6440 – paniym – Strong's Hebrew Lexicon (NASB)." Blue Letter Bible. Web. 16 June, 2020. <https://www.blueletterbible.org//lang/Lexicon/Lexicon.cfm?Strongs=H6440&t=NASB>.

5. "H8415 – tehowm – Strong's Hebrew Lexicon (NASB)." Blue Letter Bible. Web. 16 June, 2020. <https://www.blueletterbible.org//lang/Lexicon/Lexicon.cfm?Strongs=H8415&t=NASB>.

6. Ibid.

7. "H1949 – huwm – Strong's Hebrew Lexicon (NASB)." Blue Letter Bible. Web. 16 June, 2020. <https://www.blueletterbible.org//lang/Lexicon/lexicon.cfm?Strongs=H1949&t=NASB>.

8. "H7307 – ruwach – Strong's Hebrew Lexicon (NASB)." Blue Letter Bible. Web. 16 June, 2020. <https://www.blueletterbible.org//lang/Lexicon/Lexicon.cfm?Strongs=H7307&t=NASB>.

9. "H430 – 'elohiym – Strong's Hebrew Lexicon (NASB)." Blue Letter Bible. Web. 16 June, 2020. <https://www.blueletterbible.org//lang/Lexicon/Lexicon.cfm?Strongs=H430&t=NASB>.

10. "H7363 – rachaph – Strong's Hebrew Lexicon (NASB)." Blue Letter Bible. Web. 16 June, 2020. <https://www.blueletterbible.org//lang/Lexicon/Lexicon.cfm?Strongs=H7363&t=NASB>.

11. Ibid.

12. "H559 – 'amar – Strong's Hebrew Lexicon (NASB)." Blue Letter Bible. Web. 17 June, 2020. <https://www.blueletterbible.org//lang/Lexicon/Lexicon.cfm?Strongs=H559&t=NASB>.

13. *R.T. Kendall,* Understanding Theology, *Vol. 2 (Ross-shire, Great Britain: Christian Focus Publications, 2000), 178.* https://answersingenesis.org/hermeneutics/law-first-mention-legitimate-interpretive-principle/

14. "H559 – 'amar – Strong's Hebrew Lexicon (NASB)." Blue Letter Bible. Web. 17 June, 2020. <https://www.blueletterbible.org//lang/Lexicon/Lexicon.cfm?Strongs=H559&t=NASB>.

15. "H6754 – tselem – Strong's Hebrew Lexicon (NASB)." Blue Letter Bible. Web. 17 June, 2020. <https://www.blueletterbible.org//lang/Lexicon/Lexicon.cfm?Strongs=H6754&t=NASB>.

16. "H1823 - dᵊmût - Strong's Hebrew Lexicon (NASB20)." Blue Letter Bible. Web. 17 Jun, 2020. <https://www.blueletterbible.org//lang/Lexicon/Lexicon.cfm?Strongs=H1823&t=NASB20>.

17. Stewart, Don. "Is There a Difference between Image and Likeness of God?". Blue Letter Bible. 24 Apr, 2007. Web. 18 June, 2020.

<https://www.blueletterbible.org/faq/don_stewart/don_stewart_690.
cfm>.

Chapter 10

1. "G2643 – katallagē – Strong's Greek Lexicon (NASB)." Blue
Letter Bible. Web. 17 June, 2020.
<https://www.blueletterbible.org//lang/lexicon/lexicon.cfm?Strongs=
G2643&t=NASB>.

2. "G2644 – katallassō – Strong's Greek Lexicon (NASB)." Blue
Letter Bible. Web. 17 June, 2020.
<https://www.blueletterbible.org//lang/lexicon/lexicon.cfm?Strongs=
G2644&t=NASB>.

3. Ibid.

About the Author

Susan Wells was nicknamed, "Question Box" by her paternal grandfather, Parks Bailey, when she was just a wee girl. She dreamed of being a scientist and a detective, viewing everything she discovered as "clues." Her inquisitive nature and desire to know the meaning of life and how things worked provided a natural springboard into becoming a student of the human body and eventually working in medicine.

Susan gave her heart to Jesus during Vacation Bible School in the summer of her tenth year. This was the first step in her journey of following her Savior. She learned not only to love the Word of God, but to love the God of the Word.

After raising her family, which included homeschooling her children, Daniel, Mary Catherine, and Anna, for several years, Susan went back to school to become a Physician Assistant. She now serves as a "medical detective," thereby fulfilling one of her "little girl dreams." She loves to solve a "good case."

While pastoring with her husband, Dennis, she's had many opportunities to teach and preach the Word of God. It brings her incredible joy to study the Bible, mine gold nuggets of revelation, and share them with hungry listeners.

Enjoying Grasshopper cookies, sipping a cup of coffee (fixed just how she loves it by her awesome husband), and leisurely spending time with Jesus and His Word create the perfect way to start her day. Taking a day trip alone with

Dennis to the mountains or gathering for a meal with her grown kids and grandkids are the closest things to heaven for her on this side of eternity.

If you enjoyed, *Shepherds in the Fields*, Susan would be incredibly grateful if you'd post your honest review on Amazon. Nothing fancy, just share with other readers what you liked and what blessed you.

For more insight into the "shepherding" approach to the marketplace, connect with Susan on Facebook (Shepherds in the Fields) and Twitter (@SusanBWells13). If you'd like to contact her for a speaking engagement, please visit her website, *ShepherdsInTheFields.com* or email her at Susan@Shepherds InTheFields.com.

Printed in the USA
CPSIA information can be obtained
at www.ICGtesting.com
LVHW021222240823
756073LV00005B/414